Real Estate Agent Revolution

The Three Cardinal Rules for Success as a Real Estate Agent

Copyright 2016- Michael McCord - All rights reserved

This document is geared towards providing exact and reliable information in regards to the topic and issue covered. The publication is sold with the idea that the publisher is not required to render accounting, officially permitted, or otherwise, qualified services. If advice is necessary, legal or professional, a practiced individual in the profession should be ordered.

From a Declaration of Principles which was accepted and approved equally by a Committee of the American Bar Association and a Committee of Publishers and Associations.

In no way is it legal to reproduce, duplicate, or transmit any part of this document in either electronic means or in printed format. Recording of this publication is strictly prohibited and any storage of this document is not allowed unless with written permission from the publisher. All rights reserved.

The information provided herein is stated to be truthful and consistent, in that any liability, in terms of inattention or otherwise, by any usage or abuse of any policies, processes, or directions contained within is the solitary and utter responsibility of the recipient reader. Under no circumstances will any legal responsibility or blame be held against the publisher for any reparation, damages, or monetary loss due to the information herein, either directly or indirectly.

Respective authors own all copyrights not held by the publisher.

Table of Contents

Introduction 5

Chapter One: RULE #1- Learn the Art of Real Estate Negotiation: Preparation 7

Chapter Two: RULE #1- Learn the Art of Real Estate Negotiation: Take Action 12

Chapter Three: RULE #2- Keep Your Marketing Fresh and Varied: Offline Strategies 16

Chapter Four: RULE #2- Keep Your Marketing Fresh and Varied: Online Strategies 22

Chapter Five: RULE #3- Always be networking: Preparation 29

Chapter Six: RULE #3- Always Be Networking: At the Event 37

Conclusion 49

Introduction

Well done! Thank you for purchasing Real Estate Agent Revolution: The Cardinal Rules for Success as a Real Estate Agent. At this point in your burgeoning career, you likely already read Real Estate Revolution: Comprehensive Beginner's Guide to a Lucrative Career and are ready to take your new endeavor to the next level! Congratulations! True success in real estate cannot end with the basics. This multifaceted career has cardinal rules which a real estate agent should abide by to create professional triumphs and personal satisfaction. Surprisingly, many realtors ignore these rules, which is most likely evident in their mediocre results. But after reading this book, you will not settle for mediocrity!

At this exciting (and probably daunting!) stage in your career, you most likely already received your realtor license, started generating leads and have some marketing basics under your belt. Maybe you already sold your first house (if this is the case, a round of applause is in order)! But now you are ready to take your skills to the next level and to do so, you need the Three Cardinal Rules for guaranteed success as a real estate agent. This book will take an in-depth analysis of these rules and provide step-by-step directions on how to achieve your personal best.

There are plenty of books on this subject on the market, so thank you again for choosing this one. Every effort was made to ensure you will feel more competent and better groomed for real estate success.

Enjoy!

Chapter One:

RULE #1- Learn the Art of Real Estate Negotiation: Preparation

Surprisingly, new real estate agents often overlook an integral skill necessary for success: the art of negotiation. Assuring your potential clients that your negotiation skills will help solidify an agreement on their terms is a great starting point. Stating this simple sentence may reduce a client's initial anxiety and provide comfort knowing they made the right choice in soliciting your expertise. Keep in mind this is a very delicate time for both the seller and buyer: they are going through a huge life change based upon a huge financial transaction. Sure sounds scary! Here are some tips on how to succeed and provide the best service to your clients.

Get to know *a lot* about your client.

No, you don't need to know their shoe size or television preferences (unless they want a home theater!), but a truly successful realtor focuses on building a very strong relationship with their clients above anything else. High-producing agents do not have time to waste, so you should schedule a one-hour long interview with potential buyers prior to hitting the pavement. This step can save time and headache in the long run by ensuring everyone is on the same page. Make sure you get the maximum amount of information during this meeting and make sure you cover the following topics:

The motivation for buying a house: Your client may disclose information that will help guide the selection process. If your buyer is pregnant, then a neighborhood with a good school system would be a priority. If the buyer is suffering from "empty nest syndrome", then you can assume they are looking to potentially downsize. Picking up on these details demonstrate your dedication to your client and as your skills improve, you will be able to anticipate the needs of the buyer before they do!

What the buyer can really afford: Some clients become starry-eyed when they are approved for a large bank mortgage. Qualifying for a $300,000 loan does not necessarily mean they will be able to afford the monthly payments. Figuring out exactly how much your clients can manage to pay will let them know you are after their best interests, not just a commission.

Musts vs. wants: Some buyers will have a list of very specific "must haves" they want in their new home. But keeping things realistic for your client is the best tactic, instead of promising things you may not be able to deliver. Assure them you will do your very best to find the perfect home for them, but sometimes the buyer has to compromise on something. Have your client try and move things off the "must" list to a "strongly want" list. This will minimize possible disappointment or unrealistic expectations.

Out-of-pocket fees: Most likely your client has allotted money for the down-payment on their new house, but they may not be aware of the other fees involved with the purchase of their new home. Make sure you provide your buyer with a list of possible out-of-pocket expenses so they can allot for them. This includes: home inspection, appraisal, option fees and earnest money.

Family home or real estate investment: Every buyer's intention to purchase a house varies, but it is crucial to find out how long your client expects to live in the newly purchased home. Some buyers do not expect to take root and are more interested in the home's projected worth in 5, 10 years. Asking what your client's plan is can guide your research to suit their preferences.

Goals: Find out exactly what your client wants to achieve. Try and discuss the clients' goals with the other agent. Perhaps both parties would like to seal the deal within 90 days. This is a good starting point. Remember to put these goals in writing, listing all stakeholders, and include all pertinent interests.

Educate your client.

This may be your client's first ride at the rodeo. Or even if it is not, the negotiation process can be a stressful time for the buyer or seller. Mapping out a plan for your client and preparing them for possible hiccups along the way will help ease their anxiety and showcase your skills as an effective negotiator.

Prepare your client for what the negotiation process looks like: When a buyer finally finds the perfect home, they can become blinded by excitement. Or a seller may jump at an offer, forgoing any patience they had prior to entering the market. You want to reign in as much emotion as possible and be transparent with your client. Prepare them for how the negotiations are going to go so their expectations stay realistic Here is a short narrative you can use as a guide. This is formatted for when your client is the seller, but can be adapted to use towards either party.

"May we take some time and discuss what happens after a buyer expresses interest in your home? The other party and their agent put an offer in writing and deliver it to me. Here is an example of what an offer looks like (don't forget to bring a mock offer!!!) and the additional paperwork that may accompany it. There is more than just the price that needs to be negotiated. I would like to prepare you for each case scenario so we can all move forward with confidence."

Prepare your client for the worst case scenario: Unfortunately, real estate agents cannot perform miracles (though darn close!), and you must be honest with your client. Present to them not only the best but also possible worst case scenarios. This may seem counterintuitive, but you are creating your client's expectation for how it will go. Remember, this is a life-changing decision for your client. They don't need surprises and being upfront showcases your integrity. But be sure to let them know your hard work and attention to detail will help secure the best deal possible.

Chapter Two:

RULE #1- Learn the Art of Real Estate Negotiation: Take Action

It's action time! Enter this stage with confidence and get excited. This is where your skills as an outstanding real estate agent will be exhibited. Keep in mind that the art of negotiation is a learned skill, and it can feel uncomfortable at first but will improve with practice. Keep the following hints in mind and apply when necessary.

Keep the boxing match to two rounds only: Insightful real estate agents realize the buyer and seller should not go back more than twice when negotiating the sale. During the first series of negotiations, the two parties are only concerned with buying or selling the home. In the second round, the focus shifts almost completely to money, where emotions escalate. Any negotiations at the third round can create resentment between the two parties, and at this point the chances of the buyer and seller coming to an agreement drops to almost zero.

Do not insult the other party: No matter how irritated you become towards the other real estate agent or party, remember to keep your cool. Your client does not need to take your lead and become annoyed as well. You always want to display confidence, provide comfort and continue to keep emotions regulated.

You never want to put the other party on the defensive. A great realtor knows how to effectively negotiate with the other buyer or seller, without insulting them in any way. The easiest way to start off on a really bad foot is to make a low-ball offer (usually 20% below asking). You are trying to get the best deal of your client, but keep the #1 goal in mind: to get the house. The term "turn-key" makes buyers swoon, but the perfect home most likely does not have any reason to sell below market value. Unless your client is making a cash offer, or the house has been on market for a considerable amount of time, it is best to wait for price reductions or encourage your client to bid more realistically.

Another way to insult the other party involved is presenting them a list of what is wrong with their house (usually used to justify a low offer). The seller is aware of what qualities of the property are less desirable. They do not need a list of what you don't like, as this also puts them on the defensive. There is a difference between negotiation tools and just a list of "crap".

If you must concede, ask for something in return: Let's be real: concessions are most likely going to be made. But if you are asked to give something, then why not ask for something in return? For example, if the other party wants to close in 90 days, you should say, "If we accept that, we want the patio furniture." It is a win/win because you will either get some cool furniture or the other party will most likely think twice before asking for something again.

Put EVERYTHING in writing: This is the golden rule for any business transaction. You may think oral negotiations are more personal or smaller details do not have to documented. NO. Sure, it may work some of the time, but why tempt the fates? Any misunderstandings or misconceptions (and a myriad of other problems) can halt the negotiation process and a battle ensues. Even if you have to make amend the contract five times in one day, DO IT. Just make it a natural part of your responsibility as a real estate agent.

The art of real estate negotiation is multi-faceted and is coveted skill that will improve over time. Use these tips, be confident and jump right in!!!

We learn the best from how to rectify our past mistakes. Have fun with the learning process.

Chapter Three:

RULE #2- Keep Your Marketing Fresh and Varied: Offline Strategies

By now, you are well aware of the importance of marketing. But successful real estate agents understand that the advertising world is constantly changing and evolving. Marketing should have a permanent seat on your to-do list and should always be budgeted for. If you do not maintain this investment, you will just be another mediocre realtor in the yellow pages. Well not that bad, since you have already read Real Estate Revolution: Comprehensive Beginner's Guide to a Lucrative Career, but you get the point! All forms of marketing should have one common theme: putting the needs of your customers first. Any initial point of contact needs to encourage your target audience to choose you as their real estate agent. Whether online or on paper, you need to present something unique, captivating, entertaining and user-friendly. Here are the best ways to showcase your talents, build relationships and get referrals.

Don't ignore offline tactics.

Yes! There are many ways to reach a large target audience without relying on the internet (really)! Actually, people these days often welcome other forms of marketing, whether in a mailing or local donation, to take a break from the digital world. Here are the best strategies for this type of publicizing.

Business cards: Yes, old school business cards are still effective, and you should have some on your person at all times. Actual human contact is still the best way to form a relationship with a potential client. You have a great conversation with a potential lead-- whether at a tradeshow, community event or even a bar-- and the best way to wrap up the interaction is with a solid handshake and exchange of business cards. Keep in mind, your card is the only tangible item the prospect will have, so it must be memorable. And it needs to make a great first impression on its own, because you hope the card will get passed along. Well prepared real estate agents have cards which are dynamic and UNIQUE. Someone could start a conversation about your business, just because you gave them such a cool business card. The extra investment is worth it and goes a lot further than many think.

Direct Mail Newsletters: If executed well, direct mail can be as effective in advertising as online tactics are. Your contact list should include past clients, leads and referral sources, and a newsletter is great way to keep in touch. But your goal is to intrigue your target audience, not annoy them with an unremarkable mass mailing which almost jumps into the trash on its own. Make the information you are trying to convey captivating, but reader-friendly. But what does the reader have in it for them? A truly effective newsletter will include helpful information for your audience. This could include: helpful advice for a new homeowner, neighborhood updates and topics specific to the demographic you are serving. Remember to keep your newsletter looking clean and void of clutter. You do not want to overwhelm your audience with a lot of pictures, stock photos or different fonts. A quality newsletter is printed in color and should include all of your contact information and the social media outlets you use. And here is a quirky tip: it has been proven that any form of advertisement which includes a picture of a puppy attracts more attention, which increases the chances of your target audience reading your mailing (further proving that puppies should rule the world)!

Printed letters: Yes, people still send letters in lieu of emails. Remember: in today's digital world, sending a letter feels more personal and is much appreciated. As a realtor, you should use this tactic for two reasons. First, a letter is a pleasant way to say thank you for a referral or to congratulate your client on their new home (or the sale of their home). Second, a postcard is an effective marketing tool to highlight your listings in the neighborhood. Using captivating pictures of beautiful homes lures the reader in, even if they are not in the housing market. If going the postcard route, do not forget to keep things streamlined. One listing per postcard is preferable, and you should use one your most aesthetically pleasing properties. And one last word: COLOR.

Something with purpose: People love free stuff. Successful real estate agents capitalize on this aspect of human nature. But once people acquire the free items, they assess whether or not to keep the item or throw it in the trash. You do not want to be thrown out. Make the investment to purchase custom promotional items which have your name and contact information on them. Remember you want to send your contacts an item which is useful and has a purpose, so your name will circulate through their home or office.

Here is a list of items you can mail to your clients that they will actually keep.

- Pens

- Magnets

- Calendar: To only be sent in December/early January for the following year.

- Sports schedule: In many parts of the U.S, there are sports fans who live and breathe for the team they are rooting for. For example, in New England anyone would welcome a schedule of the Patriots or Red Sox to put on their fridge. Imagine all the times your audience will be looking at your brand!

- Jar opener: This may seem silly, but you know those flat discs made out of rubber to be used to open stubborn jars? Once someone uses them, they are hooked. Throw your name and contact info on one to alleviate frustration in your neighborhood!

- The list goes on and on: The items above can be mass purchased at a very reasonable cost and will fit in a standard envelope. There are many other promotional items out there, but remember you want them to be useful.

Support a local charity or community organization: Give back to the community which literally keeps you employed. A truly invested real estate agent wants to be part of charitable events and give back to the neighborhood in which they serve. This is another way to get your name out there and connect with people on more of a humanistic level, not just business.

Chapter Four:

RULE #2- Keep Your Marketing Fresh and Varied: Online Strategies

This aspect of your marketing plan may seem overwhelming and difficult to get a handle on. This is a common misconception, but you still must dedicate time and have the savviness to get the most out of the online market. After reading this, hopefully your creative juices will be flowing, and you will feel confident with your efforts.

You may have to break up with your current website: Remember, this book is intended to take your real estate game to the next level. Dominating the online real estate market means you need to enlist a design agent who can adequately express your brand in the most unique and captivating way possible. Here is helpful information on the top real estate marking online agents who will increase your website popularity.

- WordPress Real Estate: Many successful real estate websites are created through WordPress. Many report it is extremely user friendly, and you actually own the website and which gives you all of the control. There are thousands of themes and templates to choose from, which will guarantee an exceptionally distinctive site you can easily customize and update at any time. Some themes are free, but please stay away from these, since you are looking for a truly unique experience for your audience to enjoy. The nominal fee is well worth the investment.

- WP Residence WordPress: This is the holy grail of the WordPress real estate family. It is a larger investment than WordPress Real Estate, both in time and money, but many champion realtors realize this is what helps them shine brighter than the competition. WP Residence allows your customers to tag favorites and save searches. There is also an email alert feature which is great for lead generation and will keep your site viewers in the loop. And perhaps most importantly, users can register and login from their Google, Outlook, Yahoo or Facebook account, which is fantastic for Facebook advertising.

- Ixact: This marketing agent helps you create a real estate website which offers three marketing tools managed from a single dashboard. Many users report Ixact is easy enough for novice realtors to maneuver and easily grows alongside the increasing success of the agent. The tools Ixact provide include Customer Relationship Management software, Content Relationship Management software, and automated email marketing. Ixact also analyzes your email traffic and will report your email open rate, click-through rate and how many recipients are forwarding your emails. It also reports what parts of your website received the most attention, which hyperlinks are being used the most and how many viewers visit your site each day. Ixact is the most expensive service of the three, but is the most comprehensive and well worth the investment as you climb the ladder of real estate success.

Search Engine Optimization: As a refresher, Search Engine Optimization (SEO) is the process of optimizing any website in order to increase the non-paid and non-sponsored traffic from search engines such as Google, Bing, and Yahoo. Real estate SEO will literally put your website at the top of the list. Large online real estate brands like Trulia and Zillow usually dominate the search engine scene. But great real estate agents will put in the time and effort to make sure their SEO is always on point. SEO can be an intimidating and complex endeavor, but here are great tips to get you on your way. Keep practicing, and you will be pleasantly surprised with the amount of traffic you continue to generate.

- Research keywords: In order for a search engine to find your website, you must pick relevant keywords or phrases your target audience would use while searching for their dream home. An easy way to do this is through Google Keywords which will suggest long keywords to include in your website which will in increase your SEO. Build your content around these phrases, and you can also find out if any other local realtors are using the same keywords.

- Local traffic: Generating nationwide search engine traffic is pretty useless, unless you are ready to expand throughout the United States. And if this is the case, then you should probably but this book down and get back to work! You want to attract prospective clients on a local level, while optimizing your audience. Add local content to your website like related businesses, community calendars or landmarks in your area. Partner up with other organizations and share website links which will start a chain in search listings, constantly expanding your audience.

- Keep your content fresh, relevant and always be increasing your site content: Mediocre real estate agents may create a great website, but then leave it to rot in the search engine wasteland. Your initial SEO efforts may initially be rewarding and boost your search engine ranking. But remember that rankings are constantly fluctuating and new information is continuously being introduced to the world. So in order to remain at the head of the pack, you must keep your site content current, varied and user-friendly.

- Use eye-catching, modern and clear images throughout the site: The use of pictures and images are imperative to a successful real estate website and is a great way to improve your SEO. Your images need to sell the house. So using poor quality pictures express that you have poor quality properties to offer. Using the right image can complement and also enhance what you are offering the consumer. Do not forget to include a description of the pictures, including keywords to generate a higher SEO. And if you really want to knock the socks off your site visitors, impress them by using a drone to take your photos. This may sound like an extravagant cost but with its increasing popularity, drone photography has become an affordable and accessible option for real estate agents who want to take their brand to the highest (literally!) level.

- Be patient and look towards your bright future as a realtor: Frankly, Search Engine Optimization demands a lot of time, effort and patience. A successful real estate agent will always be in the process of SEO for their website. Remember you may not see any progress for a while. Your website will not even be a twinkle in Google's eyes until you consistently produce quality information and remain diligent, no matter what. Average realtors eventually quit the process, because they are impatient and pull out before seeing results. So optimizing your SEO will naturally weed out your competition without any extra effort on your part.

Make sure your site is mobile: More than 85% (!!!!) of new home shoppers use their phones during the purchase process. There has been more than a 300% increase of real estate related searches on tablets (like Kindles) over the past two years. Be absolutely positive your website propagates correctly on mobile devices, or your SEO efforts will be wasted, and your potential buyers will go find a more user-friendly realtor site to peruse.

Exemplary real estate agents always make sure their marketing tactics are current, constantly evolving and showcase their talents in the best way possible. You are your own brand, so putting your best foot forward on any platform is imperative for real estate success.

Chapter Five:

RULE #3- Always be networking: Preparation

Let's take a moment for you to pat yourself on the back for getting this far in the extremely rewarding and multi-faceted profession of real estate. As you know by now, a successful realtor is always thinking about how to keep thriving in this competitive arena. Many real estate agents believe networking is the #1 way to stay above the pack and dominate your target area. There are many ways to network, and you must make the most out of every opportunity that comes your way. At this point as a realtor, you are ready to expand your audience from consumer (the buyer/seller) to other professionals in your industry in order to expand your knowledge (NEVER stop being willing to learn) and grow your business. There are endless network opportunities in the real estate arena, and professional events are very easy to find. The more you get out there, the more comfortable you are going to feel which will boost your confidence and success. And most importantly, remember to keep having fun. Meeting liked-mined people who are driven by their love of the profession can be really inspiring. Take it all in.

How to find meet-ups and professional events.

Yes, it can be as easy as Googling "professional networking events in my area." You would be surprised at how quickly you can find and assess what events would be most helpful for you to attend. Here is a list of websites which host professional events all over the United States to narrow down the field.

- Meetup: Meetup is the #1 website where real estate professionals go to find the best networking platforms in the industry. People gather who have matching interests and goals which makes it very easy to build more connections. You also have the power to create your own professional meetup through this site.

- Eventbrite: Your first visit to this website will delight you, as networking opportunities in your exact location fill your home screen immediately. There are countless organizations, associations and conferences listed for you attend, and you can even pre-register for many of them directly from the site. And similar to meetup.com, you can organize your own event through Eventbrite.

- LinkedIn: You have already set up a LinkedIn account and have been generating leads in this online environment (right? RIGHT?), but you can find and host real-life events in your area through this website as well. Users easily choose their industry and location to generate results, but keep in mind LinkedIn usually only highlights events in major cities.

- Netparty: Let me warn you—Netparty's logo is a martini glass with the tagline: "Networking with a twist." So, this networking host is geared towards a very specific audience in a less formal environment. Its aim is to bring young professionals (usually in their 20's to 30's) together to attend fun, stylish and sometimes glamourous events in their area. These events are not hosted in stuffy conference halls, but instead in upscale clubs, rented mansions and fancy lounges. Why not give it a shot???? If anything, you will have a night out you will not forget.

- Craigslist: Yes, Craigslist is still a reputable website which continues to be the leader of the pack in heavy online traffic. It offers a very easy way to find a large variety of events in your area, most of which are free. Craigslist also provides events which may be on the unconventional side, further expanding your network.

- Dames Bond: That is not a typo. Dames Bond is an all-female community (sorry guys!) with the goal to empower and connect women wanting to dominate the business industry. Forbes even named this website one of the Top 10 Career Sites for Working Women, so the results are undeniable. You can easily find meet-ups and professional events in your target area, and Dames Bond also offers schedules for educational and motivational lectures to keep you curious and inspired.

Create a strong presentation.

Okay, we are going to talk about how to create a presentation which will delight, educate and effectively convey your brand to the target audience. At smaller, more formal networking events, you may be granted the opportunity to give a presentation on what you have to offer to the industry of real estate (and remember, you have a lot to offer!!!). Even successful realtors can lose credibility if they give an ill-prepared presentation to their peers. Public speaking is learned skill, and one most people are not comfortable with. So do not worry if this aspect of the job daunts you, because that is completely normal. But if you have a thoughtful and comprehensive presentation created, it will guide you through your fears and build your confidence. The people in your audience may not remember everything you said, but they will remember YOU if your slides are dynamic, eye-catching and unique. A slide show consists of graphics, text, videos and charts to simplify what you are trying to convey to your audience and keep them entertained throughout. Here is a list of the best real estate presentation tips to take your game to the next level and help your brand dominate the market.

What makes for a great presentation: Sometimes it is a challenge to sort out what you want to convey to your audience in the most efficient and aesthetically pleasing manner. Here is a list of ways to accomplish this like a pro.

- Be data driven: In many instances, you will not be allotted a lot of time to present. If this is the case, your presentation must quickly identify your strengths, including the data to back them up. This can be conveyed effectively with a history of your successes and any other accolades or facts you want to include.

- Use charts and graphs: Remember, you want to express your intentions in the clearest, most efficient way possible. To do so, try and limit the amount of text you use and incorporate charts and graphs instead. You can really do this with anything but just remember to keep it purposeful. No one wants to listen to pointless dribble just to use a pie chart.

- Stay modern: The top real estate agents will keep their presentations fresh and professional while captivating the eye. Today's most effective networking presentations include photo-rich slides which tell a story even without narration. Popular sites like Pinterest are based upon visuals, and this trend has not slowed down. But remember to keep the standards of the photographs you use HIGH. Poor quality shots will work against you.

Don't go it alone: Brace yourself. DO NOT USE POWERPOINT. There are plenty of more modern real estate presentation tools out there that will help you captivate your audience without relying on the outdated PP. Don't let this scare you though. Here is a list of great websites which will help you create that fresh and highly memorable presentation.

- Prezi: Though Prezi has been around for years, its popularity has recently skyrocketed because people finally became tired PowerPoint. There is a slight learning curve, but the results are impressive. Prezi also includes a zoom feature which is new and unique. Recommended for people who are used to PP and ready to take things up a notch (or ten!)

- Canva: Canva is arguably the most popular real estate presentation tool out there. It is geared towards users on all levels, even people who aren't too tech-savvy. Canva offers a large number of design and data formats, which you can easily plug in your data into. There is also a large library of images, stock photos, fonts and icons you can drop into your presentation easily. The results are beautiful will still being content-rich.

- Slidebean: Raise your hand if you already made a PowerPoint presentation. That's okay, and kudos for putting in the effort. Thank the realtor Gods that there is an online tool which can convert your already constructed PP slides into a visually updated presentation. Slidebean boasts ease of use and even claims to be more use-friendly than PP.

- Haiku Deck: This presentation service claims you will have lots of fun while constructing your slides through their site. Most of the templates they offer are very elegant and upscale looking. Any agent looking to be remembered should keep Haiku Deck in their arsenal.

- Google slides: For whatever reason, people take comfort when using anything Google has to offer. Many realtors report that Google Slides has the familiarity of PowerPoint but produces a higher quality product. You can work on your presentation offline, and it auto saves everything so you don't have to worry about losing your work in the big dark pit called the internet.

Chapter Six:

RULE #3- Always Be Networking: At the Event

You got this. Up to this point, hopefully you feel better prepared to make an indelible mark on the real estate networking scene. It's time to put your best foot forward (in a freshly polished shoe) and take advantage of all that a networking event has to offer. Read and really practice the advice below.

It's showtime.

Get to the event early: A driven and productive real estate agent takes advantage of every opportunity given to them. Time is of the essence, and by now you understand the depth of the commitment necessary to thrive in this industry. If you get to the event early (and other people will too), this allows you to get to know a couple people before the rest of the pack even arrives. This maximizes your time and increases your network. Also, if you arrive late (that word should be erased from your vocabulary), the other attendees will already have formed groups and will be engaged in conversation. At this point, it will be much more difficult to ease your way into a discussion.

Smile: Seems intuitive, but often our nerves dominate our appearance. People want to feel like you are genuinely interested to meet them and want to glean from their experiences-- not just going through the motions. BUT don't keep a fake, plastic smile on your face until your cheeks hurt. A successful realtor looks genuine and at ease with all they do.

Position yourself effectively: Think about the last conference or event you attended where food was served. Everyone loves free food. Stand near the appetizer table or where they serve drinks. Look casual. People feel less inhibited when they are eating. A little plate of food or a drink in your hand can give you something to do if conversation lulls.

Quality, not quantity: A successful real estate agent doesn't set out to meet everyone at the event. Remember you are looking to form relationships with people and not be a networking robot. Meeting 5-6 people is a good number, as long as each interaction is meaningful. Also, this will make it easier for you to reference conversations you had when you follow-up.

Do not disregard the wallflowers: So, out of a room of 50 people, which 5-6 people do you want to introduce yourself to? Remain aware of the wallflowers and those who are standing on the periphery of the room. More times than not, this is where the heavy hitters in the industry position themselves. This is your chance to approach an organization leader or even the person who funded the event. Strategy is HUGE.

Go for it: If you see someone you would like to network with, put on a warm smile and introduce yourself (don't forget the solid handshake). You can simply say, "Hi, my name is Chris from ABC Real Estate, pleased to meet you," or, "Hi, I don't know many other people here, so I would like to introduce myself," and go from there. Keep in mind, people will probably be relieved you took the initiative to approach them, and no one has ever replied, "No, I do not want to meet you." Here are some straightforward, all business conversation starters:

- "What brought you here today?"

- "How did you hear about this event?"

- "Why did you decide to enter real estate?"

- "Do you find real estate as rewarding as I do?"

- "Competition is rough these days. How do you try to stand above?"

But some networking events have more of a social vibe, so the conversation starters above may turn people away. Use any of these more relaxed, light-hearted approaches... the list is endless! Some of these may seem intuitive, but it is important to keep ice breakers in the back of your mind at all times. Nerves make it more difficult to sound natural, and sometimes the simplest things can be botched.

- "How has your week been so far?" This is more effective than "How are you," because it invites more detail.

- "Have you been to this venue before? It's really nice!"

- "What do you think about the (food, weather, sports team, etc)?"

- "Are you freezing (or warm) too?" Perhaps your body temperature is perfect, but it prompts the person to answer, and then a connection is made.

- "Are you local? How long did it take you to get here?" This is especially helpful if the event is located in a city, as people love to vent about traffic.

- "Can you believe what is happening with (major news story)?"

- "This event is great; don't you think?"

- "I'm a little nervous, how do you look so comfortable?" People appreciate it when someone else exposes their vulnerabilities. This makes an instant human connection.

- "Can you believe (holiday, season) is right around the corner?"

- "Is the wine here that bad, or is it just me?"

- "Have you seen any of the real estate reality TV shows? Aren't they awful?" (because they are!!)

- "Are you familiar with this area? I wanted to grab dinner here before heading home."

- "What are the worst conversation starters, so I don't use them?"

- "I sometimes feel like we are speed dating at these things!"

But keep in mind you are not at a bar, trying to pick up a date. Sometimes using less formal ice breakers can sound creepy instead of light-hearted. Be comfortable, but remember this is still a professional event, and you are there to make the best impression possible.

*Always try to give **sincere** compliments*: People love being complimented for really anything. But the only way to be effective is by being sincere with what you are saying. Compliment the person with something that you actually like about them. You like their boots? Say it. Are they wearing a great color? Tell them. Are they wearing a neat tie? Praise it. Remember to follow-up the compliment with a question, so the conversation doesn't die (I couldn't help but noticing your necklace, where did you get it?").

Never talk negatively: Sure, sometimes it is easy to make a connection with someone based upon negative talk. You could take a chance and say to someone, "Wasn't that last speaker boring?" or "Sometimes these events are such a drag, don't you think?" But then what happens when the person thinks the opposite? Or if the person is the best friend of the last speaker? Well, you just made a connection, but a detrimental one. Or you will be a real buzz kill. Successful agents always stay positive and complimentary.

The meat of the interaction.

Now that you are completely engaged in conversation with someone, it is time to really test your skills as a top networker. The definition of network as a verb is, "interact with other people to exchange information and develop contact to further one's career." Sounds pretty on point. But power real state networkers take it to the next level. A true master has the ability to relate well with others and has the skill to form meaningful interactions in a short amount of time.

Listen more than you talk: Be aware of how many times you say "I" in a conversation. You want to generate meaningful conversation and keep the focus on the other party. No one wants to listen to a know-it-all, or someone who won't shut up about their personal achievements. You want to stay vigilant with what the other person is trying to convey and allow them to do so. If you actually listen and stay focused, you can really learn a lot about the other person, and in this case, a lot about their business. And surprisingly, people will remember you and the conversation better if they talk more about themselves. But don't forget to get your point across and goals met!

Get personal, but not too personal: You want each interaction to be valuable and gainful, but personable without being inappropriate. Again, you want to avoid being a networking robot. Seasoned realtors know how to intertwine business with personable banter. If the other person mentions a spouse, ask what they do for a living. If they say they used to work in a different region or state, ask why they relocated. This keeps conversation flowing and a great way to make your interaction more meaningful.

Be aware of your nonverbal cues: Many researchers argue that 93% of all communication is nonverbal. To break it down even further, 55% is body language and 38% is tone of voice. Whether or not these statistics are true, nonverbal cues and how you present yourself sans words is EXTREMELY important. Here are some ways on how to stand out in the crowd without even speaking.

- Keep your shoulders back and head held high. This displays confidence and poise.

- Nod when the person takes a pause in their story or when you should agree with something they are saying. This shows that you are actively listening, and they have your attention.

- Make eye contact.

- Have open body language. Do not cross your arm across your chest. Even if you are cold, it gives the impression you are closing off the other person or in disagreement with that they are saying. Also, shifting your body slightly outwards allows other to join the conversation with ease, if that is what you want.

How to wrap things up.

You never want to rush through a conversation, but you also want to optimize your time and hit your 5-6 target people. If you are engaged in a lengthier conversation because it seems fortuitous, don't hesitate to stay with it. Intuitive real estate agents know the right time to start ending the conversation appropriately and efficiently. Trying to have a positive lasting impression is important, and is a skill in itself. Successful realtors keep exit strategies at hand in order to wrap things up politely and effectively.

Sometimes things are awkward: You never want to get trapped by one person for too long which will result in missed networking opportunities. If there is an uncomfortable lull in the conversation, this is a great time to wrap things up. You could say, "I hope your project goes well, let me know how it goes?" This shows you have been listening to their story and gives you the opportunity to exchange contact information.

Sometimes things are painful: Yes, you will often run into people who have no interest in what you have to say, are just there to complain about the industry or are downright rude. Do not waste your time or even exchange information with them. Here things to say in order to get out of the conversation ASAP, while doing it cleanly and respectfully.

- "I'm going to go grab another drink, thanks for your time."

- "I see a colleague of mine whom I haven't seen in a long time. Take care."

- "I don't want to take up any more of your time. Good to meet you." (This makes it seem like you are doing them a favor by ending the conversation.)

- "I have to use the restroom." (The quickest way!)

Exchange business cards with ease: It is better to ask the other party for their card before offering yours. This is a great way to express appreciation for the conversation and graciousness. And when they hand it to them, make sure you glance at it and don't just stuff it in your pocket. Again, another way to make your interaction more genuine. At this point, the other person will most likely ask for your card in return. If this isn't the case, you can say, "Oh, and can I give you mine?" It is that simple.

Stay upbeat to the very end: Have the last thing you say be cheerful and optimistic. You could say, "This was a great conversation, Ted" "It was such a pleasure to meet you, Lauren" "Good luck with everything, Jon!"

Follow-up (duh).

It is CRUCIAL to follow-up and do it in a TIMELY manner. You just put your best foot forward and impressed many fellow networkers. This is the foundation of the relationship, and now it is time to build upwards and keep the connection meaningful. You could send an email, letter or any other marketing tactics explained under Rule #2. Remember that your already polished marketing tactics is what makes your networking the most effective. You never know when, where or how you might get a lead. And the best real estate agent always remembers to give something in return and express the upmost gratitude.

Conclusion

Congratulations! Hopefully after reading Real Estate Revolution: The Three Cardinal Rules for Success as a Real Estate Agent, you are even more excited about choosing a career in the booming and fortuitous real estate industry. Be proud you care enough about the profession and the personal development involved to be the best. Stay confident and humble. Do not be afraid to take risks. You got this!

If you follow the Three Cardinal Rules and continue to nourish the hone the skills you already have, success is inevitable. If you feel like you need a refresher course in the basics (and there is nothing wrong with this), please check out Real Estate Agent Revolution: Comprehensive Beginner's Guide to Become a World Class Estate Agent to brush up on your knowledge.

Thank you for purchasing this book and GOOD LUCK!

www.ingramcontent.com/pod-product-compliance
Lightning Source LLC
Chambersburg PA
CBHW071828200526
45169CB00018B/1235